TAKING A BULLET FOR CONSERVATION ©

The Bull Moose Party
A Centennial Reflection: 1912 – 2012

Jim Posewitz

6/12/2018

Copyright © 2011 By Jim Posewitz

Published by Full Circle Inc.

Printed in the United States of America.

1 2 3 4 5 6 7 8 9 0 MG 17 16 15 14 13 12 11

Cover, text design and layout by Laurie "gigette" McGrath. Cover illustration by Jim Stevens.

ISBN 978-1-60639-045-0

Cataloging-in-Publication data is on file at the Library of Congress.

Distributed by
Riverbend Publishing
PO Box 5833
Helena, MT 59604
Phone: 1-866-787-2363
www.riverbendpublishing.com

Also by Jim Posewitz
Beyond Fair Chase: The Ethic and Tradition of Hunting;
Inherit the Hunt: A Journey into the Heart of American Hunting;
Rifle in Hand: How Wild America Was Saved

TABLE OF CONTENTS

ACKNOWLEDGMENTS

I greatly appreciate the time, attention, skill, and creativity contributed to this work by Laurie "Gigette" McGrath for her design, editorial, and organizational support. Likewise my thanks are extended to artist Jim Stevens for the creativity and talent he brought to this project.

Thanks are due John Organ, Harry Joslin, and Eric Nuse for their review of and comment on early drafts of this work. Thanks are also extended to Kay Ellerhoff for an outstanding job of editing that not only tidied up the writing, but also added clarity to the message.

Finally, special thanks are extended to Gayle L. Joslin for her support, encouragement, and frequent review of the developing manuscript. Her comments on both the clarity of the writing and the essence of the message are deeply appreciated.

While the mentioned participants provided valuable and needed assistance, the author retains full responsibility for both concepts and details presented in the telling of this story.

DEDICATION

This story is told to demonstrate both the fragile nature and the awesome power of the conservation ethic that emerged in our democracy. It is also told to remind us that while conservationists emerge anew in each generation, those with the passion to exploit natural resources march to a similar rhythm. Only the drummers differ.

This story is written to bring both historical perspective and encouragement to those who will carry the American conservation ethic into contemporary natural resource battles. Twenty-first century participants will determine the fate of wild things, wild places, and perhaps the earth itself.

This book is dedicated to those of you who will show up.

FOREWORD

Few ideas are as logical as the conservation and sustainable use of natural resources. Still, human history is littered with examples of their exploitation to our own detriment, and that of planet earth—our only home. Neglect is not a recent malady. In the foreword to *A Forest Journey*, author John Perlin notes that "Plato vividly warned the Athenians in the 'Critias' of the consequences of deforestation."[1] Through most of human history, decisions about how to treat nature and natural resources were made by rulers of various potency and description. When issues about respecting nature and conserving resources emerged in the New World democracy we called America, there was no precedent—and no instruction book.

America was less than a century and a half old during the presidential campaign of 1912 when a great political struggle over the conservation of natural resources was waged. On the 100th anniversary of that epic battle in 2012, it might be wise to visit that history for the lessons it holds. It is a colorful story and it includes America's Bull Moose Party, African lions, a conservation hero traveling under an assumed identity, and the near assassination of the most recent president to have his image chiseled onto Mount Rushmore. More important, lessons in the story emerge for those engaged in this century's epic struggle between man and nature.

TR carving on Mount Rushmore
PHOTO BY SCOTT CATRON Wikimedia Commons

INTRODUCTION

When our country was new, we were driven by the radical notion that people were capable of governing themselves. Seventeenth-century English philosopher John Locke articulated the idea that perhaps all men held a natural right to be "… free and equal before God and each other." Locke was seven decades in the tomb before the bold American colonists launched the Revolutionary War to win the right to test his philosophy. The American Declaration of Independence, Constitution, and Bill of Rights proudly proclaimed that human beings did not need kings, emperors, or czars to manage their lives, fortunes, or futures. The opportunities that came with independence and the right to pursue happiness were enhanced by the fact that the rebellious colonists were perched on the eastern edge of a continent blessed with bountiful natural resources. None of our founding documents mentioned fish, wildlife, forests, soil, or how a free-enterprising people were to deal with them.

The idea that "we the people" could prosper in a sustainable fashion, by using natural resources conservatively, emerged about a century after our independence was won. Embedding the idea of fish, wildlife, forest, water, and soil conservation in

9

a democratically governed society went through a monumental political struggle as the 19th century faded and the 20th dawned. The most dramatic confrontation of that epic battle occurred in 1912, and the champion of conservation of natural resources, especially wildlife, was a man with multiple identities. Soldiers knew him as the Rough Rider; to Dakota cowboys he was four eyes; to African big game hunters he was Bwana Makuba; and, to all Americans he was the Bull Moose Party presidential candidate in 1912.

In the 19th century, the crusade for natural resource conservation in America began as a plea for respecting nature. As the continent's wildlife was being slaughtered late in that century, the conservation crusade reacted to the desperate plight of fish and wildlife along with an obvious need to respect forest resources. In the third decade of the 20th century, the "Dust Bowl" and drought of the "Dirty Thirties" energized the ethic that the 19th-century conservation pioneers planted in grassroots America. In the seventh decade of the 20th century the idea spread, "Earth Day" dawned, and conservation expanded into the broader notion of environmental protection. As the 21st century unfolds, our democratic society is challenged with conserving the life support systems of the planet itself. Through this two-century span runs the need for a young nation to teach each new generation that conservation matters. As the need to reach a sustainable relationship with nature and our planet's life support system becomes increasingly urgent, our responsibility to meet these challenges likewise grows. We have met significant conservation challenges before. Time has shown us that the best gift one generation can pass to the next is the story of how it happened. What follows is a tantalizing piece of a truly amazing story.

Theodore Roosevelt "on the stump" LIBRARY OF CONGRESS

Top to Bottom:
Henry David Thoreau;
Ralph Waldo Emerson;
George Perkins Marsh.

A NATION IN NEED OF
A CONSERVATION ETHIC

When America's democracy was born of revolution in 1776, issues that fired the souls of the rebels were personal freedom, taxation, representation, and better yet—independence. None of our nation's founding documents addressed how the people of this radically new form of governing should relate to nature and the natural resources of what Europeans and European immigrants perceived to be a new world. To them it was simply an unexploited landscape untouched by "civilized" man. It was a second chance at Eden. In that context we came perilously close to becoming the most destructive culture in human history.

When our nation was young, not much attention was focused on the natural world or its protection. A French nobleman, Alexis de Tocqueville, studied democracy in America a little more than a half-century after our country's founding. The Europeans, particularly the French, were struggling with their own revolutionary tendencies and de Tocqueville wrote, "I sought the image of democracy itself, with its inclinations, its character, its prejudices, and its passions, in order to learn what we have to fear or hope from its progress." He also left us with an image suggesting that our pioneering democracy in the 1830s probably gave conservation little or no thought. He wrote:

> *"In Europe people talk a great deal of the wilds of America, but the Americans themselves never think about them; they are insensible to the wonders of … nature. Their eyes are fired with another sight; they march across these wilds, clearing swamps, turning the courses of rivers."*[2]

Seven decades later, when Theodore Roosevelt ascended to the presidency, he noted something quite similar. In his autobiography he wrote:

> *"The relation of the conservation of natural resources to the problems of National welfare and National efficiency had not yet dawned on the public mind."*[3]

Our young nation had scholars and orators calling for a more sensitive relationship with nature. Ralph

Waldo Emerson thought, lectured, and published on the subject. A mere 60 years after the Declaration of Independence, Emerson published "Nature," an essay that included a plea for the forests:

> *"In the woods, is perpetual youth. Within these plantations of God, a decorum and sanctity reign, a perennial festival is dressed, and the guest sees not how he should tire of them in a thousand years. In the woods, we return to reason and faith."*

Another early advocate for a truce, or some degree of temperance, with the natural environment was Henry David Thoreau. He remains best known for his life at Walden Pond, his philosophy of living simply, and his endorsement of civil disobedience as a means of resisting an unjust state. He addressed the need to temper our resource-exploitive tendencies saying it quite simply:

> *"A man is rich in proportion to the number of things he can afford to let alone."*

Thoreau also wrote about the value of hunting as part of our relationship with the natural world:

"When some of my friends have asked me anxiously about their children, whether they should let them hunt, I have answered , yes–remembering that it was one of the best parts of my education– make them hunters."

This latter passage turned out to be prophetic recognition of those who would introduce a conservation ethic into our America culture.

A third significant contributor to the idea of conservation itself was George Perkins Marsh. In 1800, a fire on Mount Tom, near Woodstock Vermont, burned through residual slash left behind by "cut-out-and-move-on" logging. Marsh was born a year later and grew up watching that mountain trying to emerge from its own ashes while being grazed by sheep and cattle. He also watched "… the Quechee River carry off his father's bridge and sawmill … and turn fields into useless mud flats."[4]

Politically active, Marsh held both elective and appointed government offices at state and national levels. Eventually, he was appointed Minister to Turkey by President Zachary Taylor. In that capacity, the scholarly Marsh came to realize how man had everywhere left depleted landscapes and collapsed civilizations in his wake. As he traveled the region around the Mediterranean Sea, he came to see in them a fast forward vision of America. Marsh grew up watching Mount Tom unravel and imperil his family's farm and fortune. In the Middle East he saw the eventual fate of such mountains when abuse spanned several human generations and then centuries. Marsh synthesized his wide experiences into the book "Man and Nature" first published in 1863. In time, his writings were called "epoch making" by Gifford Pinchot–the man who eventually became "America's Forester." Pinchot wrote in his own autobiography that at the time of Marsh's publication it was "...unsafe to assume...that Forestry occupied any appreciable space in the American mind of Civil War Times."[5]

Emerson, Thoreau, and Marsh all did their best to urge treating nature and natural resources with respect, appreciation, and perhaps even a little temperance. All three were born, lived their full and varied lives, and then died before Theodore Roosevelt killed his first buffalo. And when that wandering bull buffalo fell, the young Roosevelt expressed his excitement with a "war dance" of celebration around the fallen beast. He had just realized his youthful dream of being a frontier hunter.

1862 4 year old "Teedie" Roosevelt HARVARD COLLEGE LIBRARY

A TALE OF TWO BUFFALO AND A CONSERVATION EPIPHANY

The 1883 First Buffalo Kill

Before Theodore Roosevelt could eventually bring the notion of a conservation ethic to the White House, he had to find it for, and in, himself. One way to visit that time of his epiphany is to tell the story of two buffalo that he killed.

As a rather sickly youth, TR was an avid reader and adventures of the American West were a big part of what played in his imagination. Biographer Nathan Miller described the young lad as follows: "Away to the wild West! These words set Teedie's vivid imagination afire. In his dreams he escaped to the prairies and mountain ranges beyond the rolling Mississippi." The dream was persistent. In September 1883 the 24-year-old, New York State legislator, stepped off the train in Little Missouri, North Dakota, in pursuit of the rapidly vanishing wildlife of the northern Great Plains. Roosevelt feared that he might be too late

Theodore Roosevelt, "The Badland Years" LIBRARY OF CONGRESS

and in a letter to his wife he wrote that he was "…
anxious to kill some large game—though I have not
much hope of being able to do so."[6]

Roosevelt borrowed a gun capable of killing
buffalo and hired a young local named Joe Ferris to
help him find one. Only months before, the northern
plains buffalo herd experienced what turned out to be
the last major commercial slaughter, and near total
liquidation, of these magnificent animals. Theodore
and Joe hunted for days in rainy, miserable weather
with no success. They literally hunted among the
rotting carcasses of commercial slaughter's final
season. Finally, on Little Cannonball Creek, a
tributary of the Little Missouri River just inside
the Montana Territory, TR bagged his first buffalo.
His fantasy, anticipation, and the excitement of the
moment all combined to destroy any possibility of
restraint:

*"With the enthusiasm that was to be his all of
his life Theodore did an Indian war dance around
the dead buffalo, expressing his delight in every
conceivable way, in addition to giving Joe Ferris a
hundred dollars."[7]*

TR's 1889 Buffalo Kill

Six years after killing that first buffalo, Roosevelt had just been appointed to the U. S. Civil Service Commission. Before moving to that assignment he decided to return to the West for a hunt. That decision led to pursuit of the few buffalo left near the headwaters of Montana's then "Wisdom River." The search led "as nearly as he could tell" into Idaho where he encountered a small band of buffalo and shot a large trophy bull. There was no war dance this time. TR wrote of that episode:

> *"So for several minutes I watched the great, …beasts, as…they grazed…Mixed with the eager excitement of the hunter was a certain half-melancholy feeling as I gazed on these bison, themselves part of the last remnant of a doomed and nearly vanished race. Few, indeed, are the men who now have, or ever more shall have, the chance of seeing the mightiest of American beasts, in all his wild vigor, surrounded by the tremendous desolation of his far-off mountain home."*[8]

The way the still relatively young Roosevelt addressed his hunting adventures had changed. But then, much had happened to him between his first and last buffalo. In fact, he had already formed a club of like-minded sportsmen dedicated to restoration of wildlife to America.

For the sake of perspective, some estimates put the bison count at 60 million at about the time of Roosevelt's birth in 1858. When he became our president at age 42, the wild bison population had dropped to somewhere between 20 and 40 individual animals holed up in Yellowstone National Park.[9] That 42-year span of time is but a blink of the evolutionary eye.

Bison herd Photo by J.W. Meiers, Polson, MT

Theodore Roosevelt with his favorite horse, "Manitou."
PHOTO BY T.W. INGERSOLL LIBRARY OF CONGRESS

Log cabin on the Butte Ranch near Medora, N.D.
Home of Theodore Roosevelt 1883-84 LIBRARY OF CONGRESS

FINDING THE ETHIC

While engaged in his 1883 pursuit of buffalo and other big game, Roosevelt also invested $14,000 in an open-range cattle enterprise. The cattle industry was beginning to capitalize on the grass resource of the Great Plains now stripped of the wild natural grazers that had been there since the late Pleistocene. Following the personal tragedy of the deaths of both his wife and mother early in 1884, coupled with a political setback, TR returned to North Dakota in 1884 to ranch, hunt, and heal his shattered life and spirit. The setback was TR's failure to get a progressive political candidate he was supporting nominated as the Republican presidential nominee. The political setback was a portend of things to come almost three decades later, events that would lead to emergence of the Bull Moose Party. The hunting was destined to be the tough pursuit of vanishing remnants. Shortly after arriving in North Dakota, he wrote his sister,

"There is not much game, however; the cattle-men have crowded it out and only a few antelope and deer remain."[10]

A few years later, writing in his 1885 book, "Hunting Trips of a Ranchman & The Wilderness Hunter", TR left us this dramatic description of the landscape on which he was raising cattle.

> *"No sight is more common on the plains than that of a bleached buffalo skull; and their countless numbers attest the abundance of the animal at a time not so very long past. On those portions where the herds made their last stand, the carcasses, dried in the clear, high air, or the mouldering skeletons, abound. Last year, in crossing the country around the heads of the Big Sandy, O'Fallon Creek, Little Beaver, and Box Alder, these skeletons or dried carcasses were in sight from every hillock, often lying over the ground so thickly that several score could be seen at once."*

Perhaps most dramatic of all, the passage continued with the following account of a rancher's thousand-mile ride:

"A ranchman who at the same time had made a journey of a thousand miles across Northern Montana, along the Milk River, told me that, to use his own expression, during the whole distance he was never out of sight of a dead buffalo, and never in sight of a live one."[11]

These experiences were driving home the need to show some temperance and respect for the wild creatures that had fueled his boyhood fantasies. These passages dramatically described a landscape that had become the bone yard of wildlife resources described by the Lewis and Clark Expedition a mere 80 years earlier, as "…exceeding anything the eye of man had ever looked upon."

George Bird Grinnell

ACTIVATING A CONSERVATION ETHIC

Biographer Nathan Miller noted that "Roosevelt became the champion of conservation—an idea that had begun with a lonely hunt in the Bad Lands."[12] That observation was endorsed by biographer Hermann Hagedorn who earlier had observed, "Narrow notions could not live in the gusty air of the Prairies, and the Bad Lands were not conducive to sentimentalism."[13] TR's time on wildlife's collapsing frontier was crucial to his conservation epiphany. He was not alone in this line of thought. Conservation historian John F. Reiger observed:

> *"The appearance of a new monthly newspaper, the American Sportsman, in October of 1871,… was the country's first national periodical to make … hunting, fishing, natural history, and conservation its primary concerns."*

Reiger continued, *"...the enthusiastic response the journal received proves that a segment of the American public was ready for its teachings."*[14]

The original natural history editor, and eventual editor in chief of the *American Sportsman,* was George Bird Grinnell, an unabashed advocate for conservation and a powerful influence on Roosevelt. In 1872, Grinnell had hunted buffalo with the Pawnee Indians on the Central Great Plains. He traveled as a scientist with George Armstrong Custer to the South Dakota Black Hills in 1874, two years before Custer's fateful and final battle on the hills above Montana's Little Bighorn River. Grinnell made so many regular, migratory-like trips to the rapidly changing West that the Cheyenne Indians called him "Wikis," their word for bird.[15] Grinnell and Roosevelt experienced the West one decade apart, Grinnell in the 1870s and TR in the 1880s. As they shared notes and experiences, they almost certainly felt the agony of the Great Plains and its wildlife.

When the brutal winter of 1886-87 hit the high plains, open-range cattle grazing experienced a pain not much different from the agony the commercial hide and meat hunters had inflicted upon wildlife. This time the impact did not come from the guns of market shooters or the more recent cattle rustlers.

Instead it was a lesson dealt by Mother Nature. Ranchers across the northern plains lost 60-75 percent of their livestock as winter's blizzards reasserted their claim to the high plains.[16] Eight lines of poetry from "Medora Nights" say it all:

I may not see a hundred
Before I see the Styx,
But coal or ember, I'll remember
Eighteen-eighty-six.

The stiff heaps in the coulee,
The dead eyes in the camp
And the wind about, blowing fortunes out
As a woman blows out a lamp.

TR returned to North Dakota in March 1887 to survey the damage to his enterprise. According to author David McCullough, "He rode for three days without seeing a live steer."[17]

A number of really hard lessons to learn concerned both wildlife and the open–range cattle grazing that sought to replace them. As early as 1884, Grinnell had been working to create or organize an "…association of men bound together by their interest in game and fish." After assessing his losses in 1887 Roosevelt returned to New York in December and hosted a dinner party for the conservation purpose described by Grinnell. It was the founding of the Boone and Crockett Club, an organization of prominent and influential sport hunters and outdoor adventurers. Among them was Gifford Pinchot, a hunter and angler whose personal passion was forest conservation. Their immediate target was, "To work for the preservation of large game in this country... and to further legislation for that purpose."[18] Being men of action, means, and influence they quickly sought to stem disposal of the massive number of acres of unclaimed federal lands rapidly falling into the hands of corporate trusts and the notorious robber barons of that time.

Among the early legislation aggressively pursued by this sturdy band of influential people was "An Act to Repeal Timber Culture Laws and for other Purposes..." This 1891 act revised the existing land laws and granted U.S. presidents authority to withdraw timber lands from the public domain and make them "forest reserves." The purpose was to bring them under the protection and management of the federal government. The act was also known as the "Creative Act." The immediate result was relatively modest use of the act to create or establish forest reserves around the perimeter of special places like Yellowstone National Park. The American conservation ethic had a foothold, but it would take something spectacular to spread that ethic into grassroots America still pioneering its way across the nation's landscapes. Something pretty spectacular was at hand!

Winter in the badlands, Theodore Roosevelt National Park.
NATIONAL PARK SERVICE PHOTO

Theodore Roosevelt and the "Rough Riders." LIBRARY OF CONGRESS

THE RISE OF THEODORE ROOSEVELT

Nobody doubts that Theodore Roosevelt was politically ambitious, but perhaps the North Dakota cowboys were the first to suggest that he was presidential material. TR was only in his late 20s and early 30s but something in his character hinted at his potential. Those folks living where "narrow notions could not live in the gusty air of the prairies" surely spotted it. Following an 1886 Fourth of July speech TR gave in Dickenson, North Dakota, newspaper man A.T. Packard shared a train ride back to Medora with Roosevelt. At one point Packard offered, "Then you will become president of the United States." To which TR responded, "If your prophecy comes true, I will do my part to be a good one."[19]

For TR, the trail to the White House gathered considerable momentum at the base of San Juan Hill 12 years after that train ride from Dickenson to Medora. He described the morning of that fateful day, July 1, 1898:

> *"It was a very lovely morning, the sky of cloudless blue, while the level shimmering rays from the just-risen sun brought into fine relief the splendid palms which here and there towered over the lower growth."*

When the sun set that day, the Spanish were driven from the hill, the Rough Riders were at the summit, and TR had spent what he labeled, "The great day of my life." Roosevelt believed that to be a great statesman, one had to find and meet challenges that fully tested a person's abilities. His exact words were, "If there is not the great occasion, you don't get the great statesman." Colonel Roosevelt performed exceptionally well that day and was recommended for the Congressional Medal of Honor by those who shared the field of battle with him. However, jealousies that stalked his entire political career were already emerging and the honor was not bestowed, until President William Jefferson Clinton officially awarded it in 2001, 103 years after that "great occasion."

In fall of the same year that TR led the charge up San Juan Hill, he ran for and was elected governor of New York. His list of reforms was long and Gifford Pinchot consulted with him on forestry and wildlife conservation measures that might be brought at the state level. Most public attention, however, focused on TR and an uneasy companion, New York's Republican Party boss Thomas Platt. Biographer Nathan Miller summed up the TR reforms that bothered Platt, with the list including TR's call for "… full publicity for corporation profits so the public could determine if they were excessive, the right of the state to intervene against monopoly, and the need to ensure that corporations paid their fair share of taxes." Even in 1900, that was fairly un-Republican causing Platt to suggest, "I want to get rid of the bastard. I don't want him raising hell in my state any longer. I want to bury him."[20] TR's tenure as New York's Republican governor was about to be cut short and a political pattern eventually leading to the Bull Moose Party was emerging.

Even in 1900, "burying" one of the most popular men in America was not a simple task. The strategy selected was to induce TR to be the vice presidential candidate on the William McKinley for president ticket of 1900. A hesitant Roosevelt initially resisted but eventually agreed. He campaigned hard for McKinley and they were elected. Roosevelt left Albany for Washington, D.C., as America's vice president. Later in his autobiography he would write, "The vice president…is really a fifth wheel to the coach…it is not a stepping stone to anything but oblivion." But then, just as our generation had a September 11th that changed everything, the fledgling conservation movement had a September day, a century earlier, that also changed everything.

On September 6, 1901, an anarchist named Leon Czolgosz shot President William McKinley. The wounded president lingered for eight days, and died September 14, 1901. The "benched" or politically "buried" Theodore Roosevelt filled the vacancy and became the 26th president of the United States, much to the consternation of one of the national Republican Party bosses. While riding on the McKinley funeral train, Ohio industrialist and party boss Mark Hanna told a newspaper editor and Republican insider, "I told William McKinley it was a mistake to nominate that wild man…I asked what would happen if he should die. Now look that damned cowboy is president of the United States."[21] Perhaps, but one thing is sure. A hunter carrying a conservation ethic was president of the United States and he was not afraid of action.

TAKING ACTION

The day President McKinley died, Theodore Roosevelt was sworn in as president of the United States. He delivered his first message to Congress on December 3rd. Biographer Edmund Morris describes a portion of that speech:

> *"Then striking a note altogether new in presidential utterances, Roosevelt began to preach the conservation of natural resources. He showed an impressive mastery of the subject as he explained the need for federal protection of native flora and fauna. Urgently, he asked that the Bureau of Forestry be given total control over forest reserves, currently parceled among several agencies, and demanded more presidential power to hand further reserves over to the Department of Agriculture."[22]*

As noted earlier, TR recognized that "…the

President Roosevelt in the White House, 1903.
THEODORE ROOSEVELT COLLECTION, HARVARD COLLEGE LIBRARY

conservation of natural resources…had not yet dawned on the public mind." The effort to change those conservation perceptions in the public mind began with his first message to Congress and eventually included seven national conferences on the subject.

A man of action as well as words, Roosevelt's administration waded into securing a public land estate destined to be a protected estate for wildlife, fish, forests, open spaces, and those Americans who value nature and outdoor amenities. For those who appreciated those amenities, it became an estate of hope. Roosevelt described a philosophy that immediately became his method of operation.

> *"I declined to adopt the view that what was imperatively necessary for the Nation could not be done by the President unless he could find some specific authorization to do it. My belief was that it was not only his right but his duty to do anything that the needs of the Nation demanded unless such action was forbidden by the Constitution or by the laws."*[23]

That philosophy, coupled with the 10-year old "Creative Act" now in the hands of one of its creators, enabled the president to get right to protecting forests, watersheds, wildlife, fisheries, and other public resources. As president, from September 1901 to March of 1909, TR compiled the following record:

• Expanded the forest reserve system from 43 million acres to 194 million acres;
• Started 30 irrigation projects;
• Saw the National Monuments Act become law;
• Created 18 National Monuments including Niagara Falls and the Grand Canyon;
• Added five new National Parks to the system;
• Established game ranges in Oklahoma, Montana, Arizona, and Washington; and,
• Established 51 Wildlife Refuges.

When the 7½-year presidential whirlwind subsided, 230 million acres had been set aside for conservation of natural resources and for Americans to enjoy. It was 359,375 square miles, roughly equivalent in size to the combined areas of Delaware, New York, Maine, and Texas. It was just shy of 10% of America. When he finished, he told us why he did it:

> *"The things accomplished that have been enumerated above were of immediate consequence to the economic well-being of our people. In addition certain things were done of which the economic*

bearing was remote, but which bore directly upon our welfare, because they add to the beauty of living and therefore to the joy of life."[24]

It worked. When those words were written, America's antelope population hovered around 5,000, now there are over a million. Wild turkeys had faded to about 100,000; they now number well past 4 million. White-tailed deer numbered about one-half million, and their population now is over 30 million. When TR was scouring remote western wild lands for elk, the nation had about 40,000; today, they too exceed 1 million and are back in Wisconsin, Pennsylvania, Kentucky, Tennessee, Michigan, and Arkansas.

Midway through America's Conservation Camelot, in 1904 Roosevelt had to stand for election to the presidency. The tension between Roosevelt and his own party that began in Albany simply escalated as TR's meteoric career carried him into the White House. The nature of that relationship was well articulated by a New York Sun editorial before the 1904 Republican Party convention. The Sun, described by biographer Edmund Morris as a "banner journal of business conservatism," editorialized: "Roosevelt steps from the stage gracefully. He has ruled his party to a large extent against its will."

The Sun's editorial then went on to single out TR's conservation record writing:

> *"And, then, there is the great and statesmanlike movement for the conservation of our National resources, into which Roosevelt so energetically threw himself at a time when the Nation as a whole knew not that we are ruining and bankrupting ourselves as fast as we can….This globe is the capital stock of the race…Our forests have been destroyed; they must be restored. These questions are not of this day only or of this generation. They belong all to the future."* The editorial concluded with a rhetorical question: *"What statesman in all history had done anything calling for so wide a view and for a purpose more lofty?"*[25]

The wonder is that he accomplished it "against the will" of both his own party and also his partisan opponents. While Wall Street and special corporate interests struggled to find ways to resist TR's 1904 nomination, he went on to win the election by the largest margin in American history up to that point. The people loved him and what he was doing for the country. Political party bosses and special interests would have to wait for a venue other than an open vote of the people to purge the reform-minded Theodore Roosevelt.

RESISTANCE

When the 1904 election outcome appeared inevitable, corporate contributions began to show up in Roosevelt coffers. One such contributor was steel baron Henry Frick who coughed up $100,000. Later when a requested favor was denied, Frick coined a phrase that still pops up in political circles: "We bought the son-of-a-bitch and then he didn't stay bought."[26] Conservation's man of principle was not for sale—not ever.

The conservation revolution that continued through TR's elected term came with considerable political resistance. Perhaps the most dramatic had to do with national forests.

In 1907, conservative western congressmen attached a rider to an appropriations bill that prohibited the president from creating any new forest reserves in six western states. TR had seven days to sign or veto the bill. Because the rider was attached

Theodore Roosevelt and Gifford Pinchot, 1907 LIBRARY OF CONGRESS

to an appropriations bill, his opponents had the votes to override a veto. TR and his chief forester Gifford Pinchot used those days, and the executive order authority that dated to the 1891 Creative Act, to create 21 new national forests in those six states. This action expanded the national forests by another 16 million acres. In his autobiography TR noted: "The opponents…turned handsprings in their wrath; and dire were their threats against the Executive; but the threats…were only a tribute to the efficiency of our action." The threats, however, were a preview of things to come.

As TR's second term was nearing an end, he sought to secure his conservation legacy by creating a National Conservation Commission. The commission's duties were to consider and advise the president on the condition and needs of the country's natural resources. He appointed his trusted friend and head of the U.S. Forest Service, Gifford Pinchot, as the commission's chairman.[27] Six months after its formation, the National Conservation Commission headed by Pinchot provided a special message to Congress that TR described as "…one of the most fundamentally important documents ever laid before the American people."

Roosevelt also sought to solidify and spread his conservation ethic and achievements by taking his message to the states. In May 1908, he convened a National Conservation Congress and most governors attended, along with 500 political leaders and natural resource experts. He launched the conference telling them, "…we have the…duty…to protect ourselves and our children against the wasteful development of our natural resources."[28] The conference was judged a success as 41 states established various conservation commissions and programs.[29] The response to the National Conservation Congress encouraged TR to organize and call a North American Conservation Congress. It assembled on February 18, 1909, and included Canada and Mexico. It met in the White House for five days and Pinchot again served as one of the commissioners. TR's time in office was now in its final weeks and he was doing everything possible to create conservation momentum. Congress, however, failed to provide for continuance of these commissions and actually passed "…a law to prevent the Executive from continuing the commission at all."[30]

In the 1908 election, Roosevelt endorsed fellow Republican William H. Taft, based on assurance from Taft that he was in sympathy with Roosevelt's reforms. However, after the election Taft replaced all of Roosevelt's cabinet. In his autobiography, TR took note of the escalating political hostility: "When my successor was chosen…leaders of the House and

Senate ... felt it was safe to come to a break with me."
Roosevelt went on to say that there were contests,
"...quite as bitter as if they and I had belonged to
opposite political parties."[31] Change was at hand and
things were going to get rough.

While the anti-conservation political maneuvering
bothered TR, his focus was somewhere else. He spent
the last day of 1908 testing his rifles for his African
hunting trip noting, "Life has its compensations."[32]
The land grabbers and robber barons, frustrated by
Roosevelt's conservation initiatives, were eager to see
him off to Africa. Most of the rest of grassroots America
embraced the new ethic. They had demonstrated as
much in the election of 1904 when they gave TR
their blessing and the largest margin of victory in the
country's history.

Theodore Roosevelt, Governor Jackson, Mr. Silous, and Dr. Mearns riding in front of the engine on the way to Kapiti.
PHOTO BY KERMIT ROOSEVELT

THE CORPORATE ROBBER BARONS
<u>COUNTERATTACK</u>

Frustrated 19th-century land grabbers and robber barons were anxious to reverse the Roosevelt reforms. When his presidential term expired, TR was off to Africa, eager to pursue his life-long love of adventure and the hunt of a lifetime. He did it with characteristic flair, as biographer Aida D. Donald wrote:

> *"Clad in his Rough Rider coat and accompanied by a band playing 'There'll Be a Hot Time in the Old Town Tonight' Roosevelt sailed on March 23, 1909…Traveling with him was his son Kermit, three naturalists from the Smithsonian, a surgeon, and friends….It was the largest and best-equipped scientific safari ever to enter East Africa…"[33]*

Once again Colonel Roosevelt, TR was fully engaged. Taking the Uganda Railway to his base camp on the Kapiti Plains, he rode—perched on a seat attached to the engine's cowcatcher—that he might better observe the wildlife.[34] He was blind in one eye as a result of a sparring bout in 1904 and had limited vision in the other. Poor vision was simply something he endured all his life. Now, he was pursuing the most dangerous big game on earth. He may have suspected that bigger dangers—political beasts eager to pounce on his many reforms—were bidding him adieu from the dock. In fact, they began rooting for the lions. His departure was noted by J.P. Morgan who offered a toast, "America expects that every lion will do his duty."[35]

President William Howard Taft's accommodations to those eager to exploit the public estate created during TR's tenure were immediate. One significant change was replacing TR's conservation-oriented Secretary of the Interior James R. Garfield with a resource exploitation booster, William A. Ballinger.[36] A short time later, an Interior Department investigator, Louis R. Glavis, uncovered a scheme to transfer a block of bogus coal claims in Alaska to the J. P. Morgan-Guggenheim conglomerate. Getting no support from Interior, a frustrated Glavis took his report to Pinchot. At the time Pinchot was still serving as the head of the U.S. Forest Service and Chairman of the National Conservation Commission created by Roosevelt in 1908 to nurture or perhaps protect his conservation reforms. Pinchot sent Glavis to Taft who responded by promptly firing the whistle blower. The response also included withdrawing his support for the Conservation Commission thus allowing it expire.[37]

Pinchot never dodged a fight and his philosophy and operating style embraced public exposure and a trust in the people. At one point he counseled his forest supervisors to follow his lead and "…use the press first, last, and all the time if you want to reach the public."[38] When the conservation dominoes started falling, Glavis and Pinchot told magazines and newspapers all across the country about what they considered to be a "criminal conspiracy." The scandal spilled into the open and the public outcry was immediate because the resource at stake was:

"a group of thirty-three coal claims of 160 acres each, or a total of 5,280 acres, in the Bering River coal field…. The actual value of the…claims was estimated all the way…to two or three hundred million dollars."[39]

Taft, furious at Pinchot's media campaign, fired

him on January 7, 1910. Ten days later, a native runner brought the news to Roosevelt who was hunting white rhino in the Congo. "I cannot believe it…," TR wrote Pinchot. "I do not know any man in public life who has rendered quite the same service you have rendered…." In a second letter Roosevelt wrote, "…I cannot as an honest man cease to battle for the principles for which you and I…stood."[40]

Contrary to J. P. Morgan's wish that a lion eat him, T.R. was savoring his African adventure and doing pretty well against the lions. Biographer Aida D. Donald notes: "Roosevelt killed his first lion near Mount Kilimanjaro. Bwana Makuba (Big Chief), as he was called, ate the heart of the first elephant killed, as was the custom…Roosevelt himself killed 9 lions."[41]

OUT OF AFRICA AND BACK
<u>INTO THE ARENA</u>

In March, to J.P. Morgan's disappointment, Bwana Makuba came out of Africa. The lions had failed to do their duty and eat him as urged by Morgan. The score was in fact TR nine—lions zero. TR entered Africa riding the cowcatcher of a steam engine train. When time came to leave, he rode a steamer down the White Nile River. The press, aware of his imperiled conservation reforms, was waiting with the big question, "Would he run for president in 1912?"[42] Some reporters were so anxious for news from him that they raced up the White Nile in launches to meet him. Bwana Makuba was coming out of Africa and the whole world was watching and listening. But first, Roosevelt, who was probably the most popular man in the world, would tour Europe as he had planned.

In late March, Gifford Pinchot boarded the SS

President Grant in New York harbor and sailed for Hamburg, Germany. To avoid media attention to his coming rendezvous with TR, Pinchot traveled under the name Gaylord Smith. On April 10, 1910, in Porto Mauritzo, Italy, two of America's greatest conservationists reunited. There was much to discuss. Pinchot's diary noted: "...one of the best and most satisfactory talks with T.R. I have ever had. Lasted nearly all day, and till about 10:30 at night."[43]

The conversation with Pinchot likely included a plea that Roosevelt seek the Republican nomination for president in 1912. Two weeks later, on April 23, TR's answer was not too subtly hidden in a speech that he gave at the very old and prestigious French University, the Sorbonne in Paris, calling it "...the most famous university of medieval Europe at a time when no one dreamed that there was a New World to discover." The speech contained what have become Theodore Roosevelt's most famous and memorable lines:

"It is not the critic who counts, not the man who points out how the strong man stumbled, or where the doer of deeds could have done better. The credit belongs to the man who is actually in the arena; whose face is marred by the dust and sweat and blood; who strives valiantly; who errs and comes

up short again and again, because there is no effort
without error or shortcoming; who knows the great
enthusiasms, the great devotions and spends himself
in a worthy cause; who at the best, knows in the
end the triumph of high achievement, and who, at
worst, if he fails, at least fails while daring greatly;
so that his place shall never be with those cold and
timid souls who know neither victory nor defeat."

It seems probable that he was offering the hope that he was about to re-enter the arena to defend his reforms. On June 18, 1910, what was then the largest crowd in the history of New York City welcomed him back into the arena. A writer of verses at a U.S. humor magazine of the time noted his return with the following poem.[44]

Teddy, come home and blow your horn,
The sheep's in the meadow, the cows in the corn.
The boy you left to tend the sheep,
Is under the haystack fast asleep.

Harpers Weekley *1912*

1912—THE BULL MOOSE IS BORN

By spring 1912, Theodore Roosevelt's hat was tossed into the political arena. Two other Republican candidates were seeking the nomination: the incumbent president William H. Taft, and Robert LaFollette of Wisconsin. At the time, 12 states conducted primary elections. TR entered all of them and won nine, Lafollette won two, and Taft salvaged only one. However, old-guard political party bosses, long opposed to Roosevelt's conservation reforms stalked their prey, not in the open public elections, but in less visible party caucus battles for convention delegates. Roosevelt nearly doubled Taft's popular vote in the 12 primary elections held. Still, old-guard political bosses were able to direct enough delegate votes to Taft to give him the nomination. They preferred a loss with Taft rather than a victory with

Roosevelt. When the vote manipulation became evident, an angry Roosevelt instructed his delegates to withhold their votes. At one point the press asked TR how he felt. In response he replied he felt strong, like a bull moose. The moniker stuck. The Roosevelt delegates then marched about a mile to their own hall chanting "Thou Shalt Not Steal" and took the first steps to forming a third party.[45] TR was thus purged from the political party of his choice. In time, the people he served would elect to put his image on Mount Rushmore beside George Washington, Thomas Jefferson, and Abraham Lincoln.

When the rebellion matured into a viable third political party, Theodore Roosevelt became the Progressive Party candidate for president. Joseph M. Dixon, U. S. Senator from Montana who also bolted from the GOP, joined TR as his campaign manager. Dixon later served as Montana's governor. The 1912 campaign was spirited and while the Bull Moose reforms ranged from a graduated income tax to the regulation of child labor, advocacy for new conservation laws was certainly among them.

AN ASSASSIN–ALMOST

On October 14, 1912, the main speaker at a Milwaukee, Wisconsin, political rally took the podium and raised his hand to quiet a wildly cheering crowd. He spoke in a low voice not typical of him beginning: "I shall ask you to be as quiet as possible... I don't know whether you fully understand that I have just been shot; but it takes more than that to kill a Bull Moose."[46] A hush fell over the arena. TR had left his hotel a short time before in an open car. While standing to acknowledge a crowd of supporters, an anti-third-term dissident, John Schrank, fired point blank into the candidate's chest. After instructing the angry crowd not to lynch the would-be assassin, Roosevelt proceeded to the rally.

Pulling his speech from his coat he noted that the bullet that had passed through his metal eyeglass case, also passed through his folded speech of 50 pages before lodging just short of his heart. When first hit,

TR speaking at Carnegie Hall . During this campaign he was shot in the chest by a would-be assassin. LIBRARY OF CONGRESS

the speaker determined that he was not coughing up blood and thus concluded that the wound would not be fatal. That was something a soldier or a hunter might know. The speaker was both. He had also been the 26th President of the United States and anchored a conservation ethic into the American culture as one of his many reforms. He was back in the political arena because he also wanted be our 28th president, not for prestige since he was already the most popular man in the world. He was back to save the conservation ethic and other reforms he embedded into our American culture from 1901 to 1909.

When the dust finally settled on the campaign of 1912, Democrat Woodrow Wilson won the presidency over the divided Republicans. TR finished second and Taft a distant third. However, the conservation ethic introduced to Americans during the Roosevelt years asserted its relevance and was strengthened by the struggle. As for TR himself, his time back in the arena was certainly "...marred by the dust and sweat and blood" just as he predicted at the Sorbonne two years earlier.

TR took a bullet for conservation on that October day. The shooter claimed his motive was opposition to anyone seeking a third term as president. However, TR probably would not have even been in the campaign had his successor honored the reforms Roosevelt had installed during his tenure as 26th President. TR was only at that rally because his chosen political party had abandoned him and his conservation reforms. In an interesting historical footnote, author Nathan Miller wrote that Shrank also claimed he was inspired by McKinley's ghost who thought TR had him assassinated and asked Shrank to avenge him. Shrank was judged insane and remained institutionalized until his death in 1940. That happened to be the same year the American people broke the long tradition and elected a president to a third term—Franklin D. Roosevelt.

The year 2012 marks the centennial of the Bull Moose Party and an exciting piece of the American hunter's conservation heritage. At this historical milepost 21st-century hunters are reminded that all political candidates have a responsibility to tell us where they stand on the American conservation ethic. It was the American conservation ethic that preserved wild places, restored wildlife to the continent, and put us in fair chase pursuit of our precious wild amenities. When we pursue a quest for political accountability in 2012, and the campaigns that will follow, we should do so out of respect for:

Theodore Roosevelt on election day LIBRARY OF CONGRESS

- conservation's philosophical pioneers like Emerson, Thoreau, and Marsh;
- late 19th-century political activists like Grinnell and Pinchot who gave substance to the conservation cause as the 20th-century dawned; and,
- Bwana Makuba, the man who stepped back into the arena in 1912 and took a bullet for us and our values.

65

Conservation of natural wonders and resources became TR's legacy.
In 1903 President Roosevelt came to inspect Yellowstone.

EPILOGUE

The current political struggle over America's natural resources continues with each new generation. In the 1912 election, the American conservation ethic was basically abandoned by the political party that once had a progressive component responsible for its birth. This political orphan, however, found a home 20-some years later when our nation was plagued by an economic depression and a drought-driven dust bowl in the "Dirty-Thirties." In the depth of those desperately hard times, conservation was once again politically embraced by a Roosevelt. This time it was Democrat Franklin D. Roosevelt. Conservation became part of the New Deal and the Soil Conservation Service and the Civilian Conservation Corps programs were among a new wave of conservation reforms.

Another critically important aspect in the emergence of serious conservation in America was the creation and support of citizen-driven nongovernmental organizations. It was a necessity recognized early by the giants of conservation who were also battling from within the government. George Bird Grinnell formed the first Audubon Society in 1886. One year later, in December 1887, he co-hosted the dinner with Theodore Roosevelt that became the genesis of the Boone and Crockett Club. When the Taft administration was capitulating to the corporate resource raiders, the recently fired Gifford Pinchot gathered like-minded conservationists and formed the National Conservation Association. The mission of this latter organization was to "Figure out how to restore the world that Roosevelt had constructed."[47] In a democracy, a pattern of individual people taking action recurs. When Franklin D. Roosevelt re-energized conservation within government in the 1930s, a similar resurgence of energy occurred in the nongovernmental sector. The National Wildlife Federation, Ducks Unlimited, The Wilderness Society, and others emerged in that difficult and dirty decade. It is how democracy works, and it may be the only way the wild things we value can be sustained from one generation to the next.

We can take a lesson from this conservation heritage story: the necessity for all of us to participate in the public affairs within a democracy. If we take time to look, history teaches us the importance of being both politically critical and also personally active. Fish, wildlife, and the clean wild places they need to survive, never had a vote. Those of us who value them have to do it for them. Let's observe the 100th anniversary of the Bull Moose Party, and the years that follow, with vigorous advocacy on behalf of America 's fish and wildlife resources. We can do it in honor of that original Bull Moose, Theodore Roosevelt, who challenged us to become the person:

> *"...who at the best, knows in the end the triumph of high achievement, and who, at worst, if he fails, at least fails while daring greatly; so that his place shall never be with those cold and timid souls who know neither victory nor defeat."*

NOTES

[1] John Perlin. *A Forest Journey*, W.W. Norton & Company, New York – London, 1989.

[2] Peter Wild. *Pioneer Conservationists of Eastern America*. Mountain West Publishing Co., Missoula, MT, 1986.

[3] Theodore Roosevelt. *Theodore Roosevelt; An Autobiography*. (a Da Capo press reprint) originally published Macmillan, NY, NY, 1913.

[4] Peter Wild Op. Cit.

[5] Gifford Pinchot (the estate of). *Gifford Pinchot, Breaking New Ground*. Island Press, Washington, D.C., Covelo, CA, 1947.

[6] Nathan Miller. *Theodore Roosevelt, A Life*. William Morrow and Company, NY, NY, 1992.

[7] Donald Day. *The Hunting and Exploring Adventure of Theodore Roosevelt Told in His Own Words*. Dial Press, New York, 1955.

[8] Donald Day. Ibid.

[9] Larry Jahn. *A Look Behind, A Look Ahead*. Wyoming Wildlife. January 2000.

[10] Hermann Hagedorn. *Roosevelt in the Bad Lands*. McIntosh and Otis Inc., 1921.

[11] Theodore Roosevelt. *Hunting Trips of a Ranchman & The Wilderness Hunter*. Modern Library Edition, by Random House,1996 (Original copyright 1885).

[12] Nathan Miller, Op. Cit.

[13] Hermann Hagedorn, Op. Cit.

[14] John Reiger. *American Sportsmen and the Origins of Conservation*, University of Oklahoma Press, Norman, OK, 1986.

[15] John G. Mitchell. "A Man Called Bird, Audubon Vol. 89, No. 2, March 1987.

[16] Clay Jenkinson. *Theodore Roosevelt in the Dakota Badlands, An Historical Guide*. Dickenson State University. Dickenson, ND, 2006.

[17] David McCullough. *Mornings on Horseback*. Simon and Schuster Inc., NY, NY 1981.

[18] John Reiger, Op. Cit.

[19] Hermann Hagedorn. Op. Cit.

[20] Nathan Miller. Op.Cit.

[21] Nathan Miller. Op.Cit.

22 Edmund Morris. *Theodore Rex.* Random House, New York, 2001.

23 Theodore Roosevelt. 1913 Op. Cit.

24 Ibid.

25 Ibid.

26 Nathan Miller, Op.Cit.

27 Char Miller. *Gifford Pinchot and the Making of Modern Environmentalism.* Island Press – Shearwater Books. Washington/Covelo/London. 2001.

28 Nathan Miller, Op. Cit.

29 Ibid.

30 Theodore Roosevelt, Op .Cit. 1913

31 Ibid.

32 Nathan Miller,   Op. Cit.

33 Aida D. Donald. *Lion in the White House,* Basic Books, New York, NY, 2007.

34 Nathan Miller, Op. Cit.

35 Aida D. Donald, Op. Cit.

36 Gifford Pinchot, Op. Cit.

37 Nathan Miller, Op. Cit.

38 Char Miller, Op. Cit.

39 Gifford Pinchot, Op. Cit.

40 Nathan Miller, Op. Cit.

41 Aida D. Donald, Op. Cit.

42 Nathan Miller, Op. Cit.

43 Char Miller, Op. Cit.

44 Nathan Miller, Op. Cit.

45 Ibid.

46 Ibid.

47 Char Miller, Op. Cit.

"A vote is like a rifle: it's usefulness depends upon the character of the user."

<small>THEODORE ROOSEVELT 1913</small>